Don't Close Your Eyes

The War Drawings

Hanna Melnyczuk

ARROWSMITH
PRESS

Don't Close Your Eyes
Hanna Melnyczuk

ISBN: 979-8-9879241-0-5

Boston — New York — San Francisco — Baghdad
San Juan — Kyiv — Istanbul — Santiago, Chile
Beijing — Paris — London — Cairo — Madrid
Milan — Melbourne — Jerusalem — Darfur

11 Chestnut St.
Medford, MA 02155

arrowsmithpress@gmail.com
www.arrowsmithpress.com

The fifty-second Arrowsmith book was typeset & designed by Ezra Fox
for Askold Melnyczuk & Alex Johnson in Perpetua fonts

Drawings in this book were done in pencil,
colored pencil, charcoal and watercolor.

This book is dedicated to the memory of my parents

Olena Zahajkewycz Melnyczuk (1921-2019)

Edward Melnyczuk (1924-2019)

And to the heroes of Ukraine

Only the dead have seen the end of war.

- Plato

February 24th, 2022: Putin's invasion of Ukraine changed the trajectory of many lives, including my own. My work has dealt with the theme of my Ukrainian heritage throughout my career. After visiting Ukraine and living there for four months in 1991, I felt very close to the people and the world my parents left in 1945. Some of my previous artwork reflects the influence of this experience. Then on February 24th came news of the war in Ukraine. In absolute disbelief, I, like most of the world, asked: "How can this be happening in the 21st century?" As the war unfolded, the images in my mind changed from being colorful representations of a child's world, stemming from my work on children's books, to darker images depicting tanks, missiles, refugees, and a mass grave in Bucha. These images continued to appear and to trouble me. I began a series of drawings based on my feelings about the war. This is a compilation of those drawings.

They expected to be home
by Spring.

But a surprise awaited them
on the other end…

Day 8 — the sky is our enemy

"Close the Sky"

Fires devoured the village,

blood poured through the streets.

Take only what is
most important.

- *Serhiy Zhadan*

Ukrainians have fled since

To know the road ahead
ask those coming back.

- *Chinese proverb*

1, 700,000 people flee Ukraine because of Putin's war.

DAY 12   (UN)

You never really
leave a place you love,
you take a part of it
with you… and leave
a part of you
behind.

- *Anonymous*

Leaving our homeland

Day 9

She saw only red.

DAY 15
March 10,
The Village Kids

He was a hero, they said.
He was my father, I said.

- DAY 19, (March 14) Mourning the Ukrainian soldier

You cry so much mother, you don't stop sobbing.

I can't see your face well, but faces don't matter much,

Your hair, I still remember, smells of cornflowers.

- *Kateryna Kalytko*

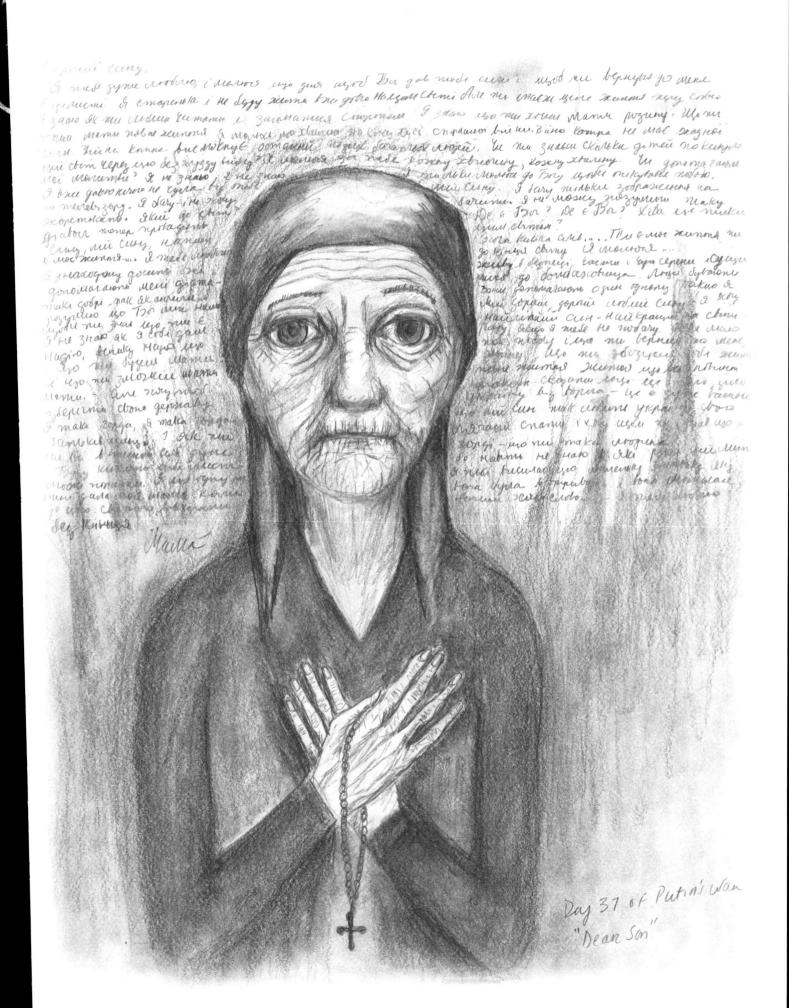

Day 37 of Putin's War
"Dear Son"

Oh, that my head were a spring of water
and my eyes a fountain of tears!
I would weep day and night
for the slain…

- Jeremiah 9:1

The soul becomes dyed
with the color
of its thoughts.

- *Marcus Aurelius*

DAY 21, MARCH 17
The Horrors of Plettin's War

There's no tragedy in life like the death of a child.
Things never get back to the way they were.

- *Dwight D. Eisenhower*

DAy 44 KramAtorsky   AbrAt 0, 50 people ded include 5 childen   About 176 have died since war

There are "new lives that already have war
in their genetic code," said Viktor Liashko,
Ukraine's Minister of Health, on social media.

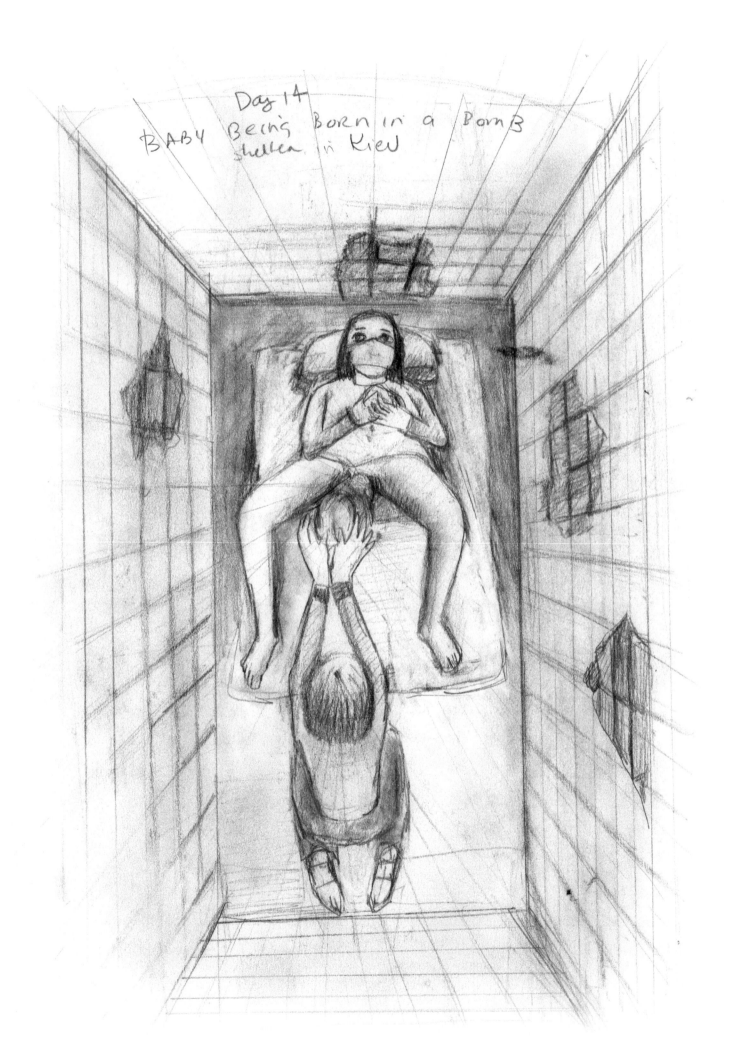

Day 14
BABY Being Born in a BomB
shelter in Kiev

Without a face

Without a voice

When I die, tell the carpenters
To take down the rafters and ceiling

- *Oksana Zabuzhko*

Day 60 of Putin's War, Apr. 124
Deborah Young Nolen

The silent witnesses

Arms made of love and steel

Day 27, of Putin's War
Why is he doing this Mama?

The essential act of war is destruction,
not necessarily of human lives,
but of the products of human labour.

- *George Orwell*

Day 32 of Palestine

Some say the world will end in fire,
some say ice.

- *Robert Frost*

Day 25 of Putin's war
March 20

After the first death there is no other.

- *Dylan Thomas*

Day 38 of Putin's War
The Red line

His body like a stone
made of feathers,
he felt it rise.

Day 46, or Putin's war

They have no voice,
only eyes that bear witness.

Yellow sunflowers
filled her eyes,
she held her breath.
Her body motionless.

Day 31 of Putin's War   Hiding

Now I see as through a glass darkly.

- 1 Corinthians 13:12

Shaking the globe
Oksana believed
she had the power
to bring her father home.

Day 3, (March 8) 3 children have died in Ukraine
and 71 have been injured   Over 1,000,000 children have left Ukraine
since the war started

Her silent scream

Whose son
are they burying
today?

Day 49 of Putin's War

GRIEF

Time does not bring relief; you all have lied
Who told me time would ease me of my pain!
I miss him in the weeping of the rain.

- Edna St.Vincent Millay

Day 40 of Putin's War

Bucha Art breakers   Massacre
400 Bodies found so far

Man is the only animal that deals
in that atrocity of atrocities War.
He is the only one that gathers
his brethren about him and goes forth
in cold blood and calm pulse
to exterminate his kind.

- Mark Twain

Day 14, March 9, 2022

Mass grave in
Mariupol Ukraine

They shall grow not old,
as we that are left grow old:
Age shall not weary them,
nor the years condemn.
At the going down of the sun
and in the morning
We will remember them.

- Laurence Binyon

Our senses, restored, never
to be the same, whisper to us.
They existed. They existed.
We can be. Be and be
better. For they existed.

- Maya Angelou

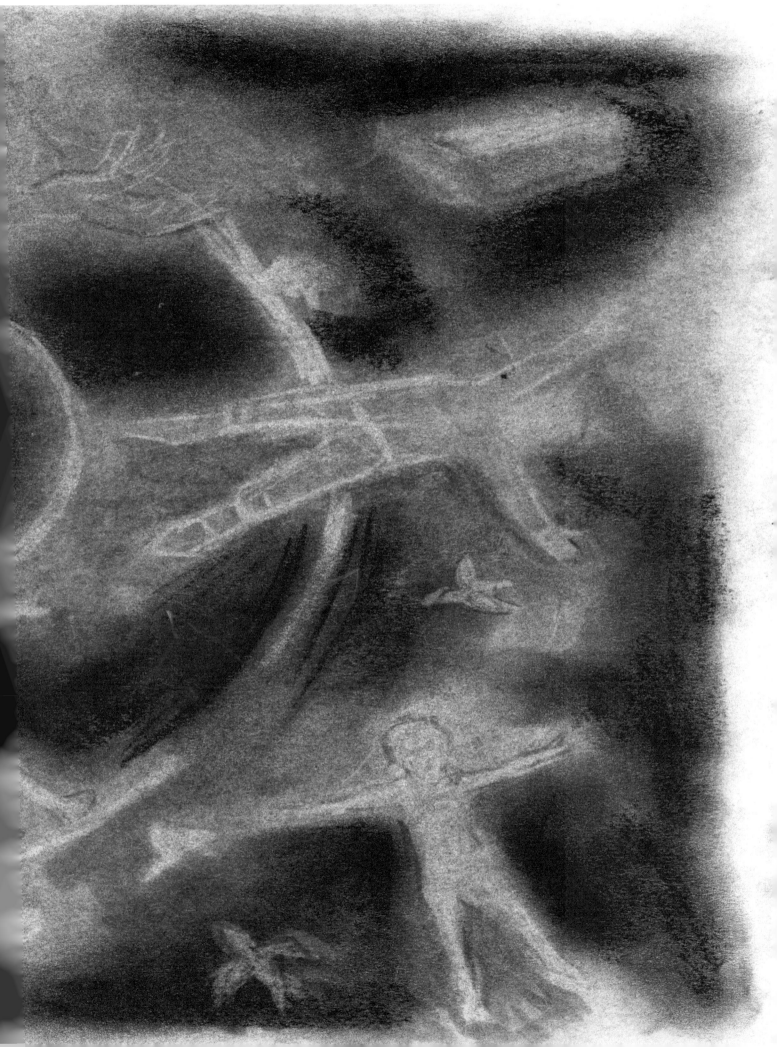

The anguish of the earth absolves our eyes

Till beauty shines in all that we can see

War is our scourge; yet war has made us wise,

And, fighting for our freedom, we are free.

- Siegfried Sassoon

Hanna Melnyczuk received an MFA from Mass College of Art. Her work has appeared at Art Space in Maynard, MA, University of Massachusetts Lowell Mahoney Gallery, The Gallery at the Piano Factory, the Danforth Museum, Tufts Gallery, Brush Gallery, Fountain Street Gallery, New Art Center, and more.

She has curated two art exhibits: Agni Magazine of Emerging Artists (published by Agni Press as *Agni 37: Standing on the Verge: Emerging Poets & Artists* alongside poetry curated by Joseph Lease and Thomas Sayers Ellis); the other, a travelling exhibit of Ukrainian artists' works, *Don't Close Your Eyes*, responding to the current war.

Hanna teaches Drawing and 2D Design at University of Massachusetts Lowell, and lives in Groton with her husband Joseph, her daughter Lara, and their cat Tello. This is her first book.

You can see more of her work at www.hannamelnyczuk.com

ACKNOWLEDGEMENTS

Thank you to my editor Askold Melnyczuk for believing in this book of images and for working with me to help the book become stronger with each revision. Ezra Fox for his amazing book design. Catherine Parnell for promoting the book. My daughter Lara, and husband Joseph for reviewing the quotes with me and offering advice and encouragement on the art and writing. Alex Johnson and Heidi Kupferman for their intuitive advice concerning images and quotes in the book, my critique and reading groups for offering encouragement and support.

To all the heroes that give up their lives so others can be free.

To my parents whose love for Ukraine has been deeply imbued in my soul.

To all the Ukrainian artists who continue to work so hard during this tragic time in Ukraine.

My deep thanks to the following publishing houses, trustees, and families for their permission in the use of the wonderful quotes throughout this book:

- Dwight Eisenhower According to the book "Random House Webster's Quotations" / Leonard Roy Frank, editor. New York: Random House, 1999. https://lccn.lc.gov/98030433, the quote comes from the PBS documentary *Ike* from 1986.

- Marcus Aurelius, MEDITATIONS.

- "When Great Trees Fall" from CELEBRATIONS: RITUALS OF PEACE AND PRAYER by Maya Angelou, copyright © 2006 by Maya Angelou. Used by permission of Random House, an imprint and division of Penguin Random House LLC. All rights reserved.

- "Absolution" by Siegfried Sassoon, published by New Directions.

- Laurence Binyon, "For the Fallen."

- Kateryna Kalytko, "He Writes," translated by Olena Jennings and Oksana Lutsyshyna.

- "A Refusal to Mourn the Death, by Fire, of a Child in London," by Dylan Thomas, from THE POEMS OF DYLAN THOMAS, copyright ©1945 by The Trustees for the Copyrights of Dylan Thomas. Reprinted by permission of New Directions Publishing Corp.

- "Take Only What is Most Important" by Serhiy Zhadan, tr. by Virlana Tkacz and Wanda Phipps, from *What We Live For, What We Die For*, Yale University Press, 2019, New Haven & London.

- "A Definition of Poetry" by Oksana Zabuzhko, tr. by Michael M. Naydan and Askold Melnyczuk, from *Selected Poems of Oksana Zabuzhko*, Arrowsmith Press, 2020.

Books by

ARROWSMITH

PRESS

Girls by Oksana Zabuzhko

Bula Matari/Smasher of Rocks by Tom Sleigh

This Carrying Life by Maureen McLane

Cries of Animals Dying by Lawrence Ferlinghetti

Animals in Wartime by Matiop Wal

Divided Mind by George Scialabba

The Jinn by Amira El-Zein

Bergstein
edited by Askold Melnyczuk

Arrow Breaking Apart by Jason Shinder

Beyond Alchemy by Daniel Berrigan

Conscience, Consequence: Reflections on Father Daniel Berrigan
edited by Askold Melnyczuk

Ric's Progress by Donald Hall

Return To The Sea by Etnairis Rivera

The Kingdom of His Will by Catherine Parnell

Eight Notes from the Blue Angel by Marjana Savka

Fifty-Two by Melissa Green

Music In—And On—The Air by Lloyd Schwartz

Magpiety by Melissa Green

Reality Hunger by William Pierce

Soundings: On The Poetry of Melissa Green
edited by Sumita Chakraborty

The Corny Toys by Thomas Sayers Ellis

Black Ops by Martin Edmunds

Museum of Silence by Romeo Oriogun

City of Water by Mitch Manning

Passeggiate by Judith Baumel

Persephone Blues by Oksana Lutsyshyna

The Uncollected Delmore Schwartz
edited by Ben Mazer

The Light Outside by George Kovach

The Blood of San Gennaro by Scott Harney
edited by Megan Marshall

No Sign by Peter Balakian

Firebird by Kythe Heller

The Selected Poems of Oksana Zabuzhko
edited by Askold Melnyczuk

The Age of Waiting by Douglas J. Penick

Manimal Woe by Fanny Howe

Crank Shaped Notes by Thomas Sayers Ellis

cont...

The Land of Mild Light by Rafael Cadenas
edited by Nidia Hernández

The Silence of Your Name: The Afterlife of a Suicide by Alexandra Marshall

Flame in a Stable by Martin Edmunds

Mrs. Schmetterling by Robin Davidson

This Costly Season by John Okrent

Thorny by Judith Baumel

The Invisible Borders of Time: Five Female Latin American Poets
edited by Nidia Hernández

Some of You Will Know by David Rivard

The Forbidden Door: The Selected Poetry of Lasse Söderberg
tr. by Lars Gustaf Andersson & Carolyn Forché

Unrevolutionary Times by Houman Harouni

Between Fury & Peace: The Many Arts of Derek Walcott
edited by Askold Melnyczuk

The Burning World by Sherod Santos

Today is a Different War: Poetry of Lyudmyla Khersonska
tr. by Olga Livshin, Andrew Janco, Maya Chhabra, & Lev Fridman

Salvage by Richard Kearney

In the Hour of War: Poetry From Ukraine
edited by Carolyn Forché and Ilya Kaminsky

A Crash Course in Molotov Cocktails: Poetry of Halyna Kruk
tr. by Amelia Glaser and Yuliya Ilchuk